THE RAMAYANA

for children

Chitra Ramaswamy

PRISM BOOKS PVT. LTD.
Bengaluru | Chennai | Hyderabad | Kochi | Kolkata

THE RAMAYANA
for children

Chitra Ramaswamy

Published by

Prism Books Pvt Ltd.
1865, 32nd Cross, 10th Main, BSK 2nd stage, Bengaluru – 560 070
Tel : 080 – 26714108 / 26703979, E-mail : info@prismbooks.com

Also at

Chennai
New No.87, Old No.5/1, 1st Floor, Jeenis Road
(Near Saidapet Railway Station), Saidapet (East)
Chennai 600 015 Tel : 044 24311244 / 24311266
E-mail : prismchennai@prismbooks.com

Hyderabad
1-1-728/A, Street No. 10, Gandhinagar,
Hyderabad - 500 080. Tel : 040 27612928 / 27612938
E-mail : prismhyderabad@prismbooks.com

Kochi
#411/3, 1 floor "Shree Parameshwar"
Muttathill lane, Kadhavanthara,
Kochi – 682 020. Tel : 0484-4000945 / 0484-2206055
E-mail : prismkochi@prismbooks.com

Kolkata
Ground Floor, D/66, Bapuji Nagar P.O,
Regent Estate, P-S Jadavpur,
Kolkata – 700 092. Tel : 033-24297957 / 24297959
E-mail : prismkolkata@prismbooks.com

ISBN 10 : 93-86506-02-5
ISBN 13 : 978-93-86506-02-3
Price : ₹95.00

Illustrations: Mohandas Marath
Ilustrations colouring artist: P.V. Sindhu
Designed at : enablePrint Services Pvt. Ltd.
Printed at: Aditya Printers, Bengaluru.

DEDICATED
to the memory of my grandparents

Smt. Ranganayaki & Sri P.R. Krishnamurthy Iyengar
Smt. Sulochana & Dr. K.S. Rangaswamy Iyengar

Lead Roles

Rama, pronounced as 'RAAMA,' Prince of Ayodhya.

Sita, pronounced as SEETA, Rama's wife

Rama's brothers are **Lakshmana**, **Bharata** and **Shatrugna**

Hanuman, pronounced as 'HANUMAAN, 'the Vanara hero devoted to Rama.

'Vanara' is Pronounced as 'Vaanara.'

Rama's other friend is **Sugreeva**, the Vanara King of Kishkinda.

Ravana, pronounced as 'RAAVANA, the Lord of Lanka.

He is described symbolically as having ten heads having strength and intelligence of ten men.

THE RAMAYANA

for children

Dasharatha, King of Kosala

Dasharatha was the king of Kosala. He ruled from the capital city of Ayodhya. With the Sarayu River flowing through it, Kosala was clean, green and had abundant crops.

Dasharatha had able ministers who helped him to rule his kingdom wisely. The People of Kosala were happy, safe and secure. They were also upright and honest, just like their king.

King Dasharatha desired to have children. He prayed to the devas for children and performed a Yajna. A Yajna is the offering made to the devas.

As the sages began chanting mantras, the flames from the sacred fire of the Yajna went up. A deva, in all splendour rose from it, a golden bowl in his hands. "Give your queens this divine payasam. They will bear you children," said the deva. Dasharatha gratefully accepted the payasam, a sweet dish, from the deva.

Birth of the princes

Dasharatha, beaming with joy distributed the payasam among his three queens. In due course of time, Kausalya, the eldest queen, gave birth to Rama. Bharata was born to queen Kaikeyi and queen Sumitra gave birth to twins, Lakshmana and Shatrugna. The birth

of the princes was celebrated with music, dance and gaiety in Ayodhya and throughout Kosala. The princes grew up under the loving care of their parents. The brothers shared deep affections for each other.

The Ashram School

Rama and his brothers were sent to Sage Vasishta's Ashram on the banks of the Sarayu. Learning in the Ashram took place in the open air, under the trees. The young boys enjoyed the chirping and singing of birds which was music to their ears. They loved being surrounded by colourful and fragrant flowers in full bloom, and watching the floating clouds and the twinkling stars.

The brothers enjoyed playing with other pupils in the Ashram. They served the Guru by doing the work entrusted to them. They learned to lead a simple and disciplined life in the Ashram.

Under the watchful eyes of their teacher, the princes became experts in horse and chariot riding, hunting, shooting, fencing, archery and in the use of various weapons. Vasishta instilled in his pupils, the importance of leading a good, righteous and virtuous life. " Princes," said Vasishta, "it is important to use the skills you have mastered, only for the good of mankind, not for causing harm to anyone."

Soon the young princes mastered the skills of warfare. They also learnt from the wise sage the art of ruling a kingdom. Their learning made them humble and responsible, well loved by all. When their training was complete, Vasishta sent them back to Ayodhya saying:

"I have taught you all I could. You must now make use of this learning in your daily life. Prove yourselves to be worthy of your father, the wise and virtuous King Dasharatha."

Vishwamitra's Yajna

The young princes returned to Ayodhya much to the delight of their parents. Soon after, one day Sage Vishwamitra came to Ayodhya to meet King Dasharatha. He told the king that he was going to perform a Yajna for the welfare of mankind. "I'm looking for brave and courageous heroes like your noble sons to stand guard while I perform the Yajna," said the sage.

A worried Dasharatha did not want his young sons to face danger from the demons. "My sons are young and inexperienced," he told the sage. "I myself will accompany you with my army."

The wise Sage Vasishta could see how Vishwamitra was keen on having Rama and Lakshmana accompany him. He advised King to send his sons with the sage, saying, "Vishwamitra is the bravest among the brave and the wisest among the wise. This is a good opportunity for your sons to learn from him."

At last Dasharatha agreed. He asked Rama and Lakshmana to go along with the Sage. After taking their father's blessings, the brothers left with Vishwamitra.

Bala and Atibala

Bow in hand, Rama and Lakshmana went with Sage Vishwamitra. They walked through forests filled with leafy green trees and gurgling streams. Sage Vishwamitra told them many interesting stories about the mountains, rivers and cities through which they were travelling. By nightfall, they reached the Sạrayu River.

The princes took a dip in river. Then Vishwamitra taught them, two secret Mantras, Bala and Atibala.

"Repeat these mantras every day. No one will be able to equal you in strength," Vishwamitra explained.

Rama Slays Tataka

The next morning, they passed through the Dandaka forest. There was a time when it was a prosperous place where people lived happily, explained Vishwamitra. They all fled when they were attacked by a dreaded ogre Tataka and her son Mareecha.

Forewarned by Vishwamitra, the brothers were prepared when Tataka charged at them raising a cloud of dust. As Rama hesitated to shoot at a woman, the Sage spoke to him hurriedly. "Rama, it is your duty as a prince and protector of people to destroy dark forces."

Now Rama was ready to take on Tataka as she charged towards him. A battle followed and at last Tatak fell.

Pleased with Rama's valour in killing Tataka, Vishwamitra taught him the use of various Astras. Astras were weapons that had the power to carry out the purpose for which they were invoked. Rama then taught Lakshmana the use these astras.

Vishwamitra's Ashram

They continued their journey through the forest. Soon they arrived at Vishwamitra's ashram atop a hillock. "I live in this Siddhashrama. This is a very blessed place because both Narayana and later sage Kashyapa performed meditation here," explained Vishwamitra.

It was nightfall when the three of them reached Siddhashram. The rishis in the ashram were happy to see Vishwamitra return with the royal brothers. They welcomed them with fruits, and asked them to rest for the night.

Everyone woke up to a bright and sunny day at Vishwamitra's ashram. The sky was clear and blue. Vishwamitra, along with other sages, began preparations for the Yajna.

As the fire from the Yajna went up, thick, dark clouds blanketed the sky. The two brothers looked up and saw Mareecha and his men approaching the hermitage. Mareecha told his men, "The sages are offering worship to devas. We shall stop them as before."

But the brothers were well prepared to counter the rakshasas. They were stopped in the mid-air as they were assailed by the missiles hurled at them by Rama and Lakshmana. The two brothers held the Rakshasa at bay as the sages led by Vishwamitra successfully completed the Yajna. Thoroughly beaten by the young princes, the rakshasas turned tail. Once again the sun dazzled brilliantly on the horizon. The Yajna was successfully completed.Vishwamitra was overjoyed. Addressing the two brothers, he said, "Your courage and bravery has made my Ashram free of these monsters."

Decision to Visit Mithila

The rishis assembled at Vishwamitra'sYajna said to Rama: "We intend going to Mithila, the capital of the kingdom of Videha. It is ruled by Janaka, an illustrious and just king. He plans to perform a great sacrifice which all of us are going to attend. We'll be happy if

you come with us. You would also get to see the marvelous bow in Janaka's court."

Vishwamitra agreed with the rishis and the decision was made. "Yes, I will take you with me to King Janaka's capital," he said to Rama. "Janaka and your father Dasharatha are good friends. They hold each other in great esteem."

Ahalya

Vishwamitra set out with Rama and Lakshmana to Mithila. On the way they came across the wonderful ashram of Sage Gautama. The hermitage, set in beautiful surroundings, was deserted. "This place is so lovely. But why is it that no one lives here?" asked Rama.

"Sage Gautama has gone to the hills to perform tapas. His wife Ahalya is very much here, invisible to us. She is engaged in penance and lives on air alone. She is waiting for you, Rama," said Vishwamitra. As soon as Rama stepped into the ashram, there was a sudden flash of brightness as Ahalya appeared before them. She looked divinely radiant and beautiful.

Meanwhile, Gautama also returned from the Himalayas. Rama and Lakshmana took the blessings of Ahalya and Gautama by touching their feet, before they resumed their journey to Mithila.

Sita

Janaka was an able monarch whom the people loved. He once desired to perform a Yagna. He selected the site for the Yagna, which he ploughed with his own hands. As the field was being cleared and prepared for the sacrifice, Janaka beheld an amazing sight!

In the middle of a trench, Janaka saw an angelic infant girl smiling at him. Janaka gently lifted the little bundle of joy in his arms and took her home. He brought her up as his daughter. He named her Sita.

Sita grew up to be a lovely young girl replete with goodness and virtue. When she came of marriageable age, Janaka wanted to find a groom who would be worthy of her. King Janaka had the heavenly

bow of Shiva which was handed over to him by Lord Varuna. No ordinary man could even move that mighty bow of Shiva. Janaka decided to give Sita's hand in marriage to one who would lift the bow and string it.

The brothers found Mithila wearing a festive look with decorations everywhere. Colourful streamers and floral toranas were hung throughout the city.

Rama Wins Sita's Hand

Janaka himself received Vishwamitra and the two sons of his friend, Dasharatha. Rama expressed a wish to see the famed bow of Shiva. On Janaka's order the bow was wheeled into the hall. It was a huge weapon kept on a carriage with eight wheels and it took a hundred strong men to bring it.

Rama looked at Vishwamitra who nodded. Rama got up, bowed to the sage and to Janaka and walked up to the his target. He bowed to Shiva's mighty bow before he laid his hand on it. To the surprise of onlookers, the next moment the bow was in Rama's hand. He not only bent it, but also broke it with ease and graceand grace. He bent it and broke it.

There was thunderous clapping and shouts of "Hail Rama, Prince of Ayodhya!" Flowers were showered on the young prince for achieving the feat with such aplomb. "I am indeed proud and happy that Sita will be your wife, Rama," said Janaka.

The Marriage

Dasharatha and his entourage came to Mithila on hearing the good news. There was music, dancing and merry making in Janaka's kingdom. Rama and Sita were married in a grand manner.

Not one, but four weddings took place at Mithila at the same time. Dasharatha's other sons also found their match here. Sita's younger sister Urmila, was married to Lakshmana. Bharata tied the sacred knot to Mandavi and Shatrugna took Shrutakirti's hand in marriage. Mandavi and Shrutkirti were both Sita's cousins.

Parashurama

King Dasharatha and the newly-wed princes left for Ayodhya with their spouses and the royal party.

On their way to Ayodhya, an awe-inspiring figure with bow, arrow and axe in hand, appeared before them. He was Parashurama.

Parashurama was the son of sage Jamadagni who had been killed by a king. Hence, Parashurama hated all kshatriyas and looked upon them as his sworn enemies. To avenge his father's death, he destroyed the kshatriyas whenever he came upon them.

Parashurama addressed Rama: "I heard you broke Shiva's bow at Janaka's court. Let me see if you can do the same with Vishnu's bow that I have in my possession! I challenge you to string my bow. If you dare to break it, I would consider you worthy to fight me!"

Rama's reply was courteous, but firm. "I accept your challenge. Give me your bow."

Rama took the bow and arrow from Parashurama. He strung it without any difficulty. Parashurama's ego was humbled as Rama strung the bow.

He reverentially bowed before Rama and left for Mount Mahendra.

There was no further delay following this encounter with Parashuma. Dasharatha and his people soon reached Ayodhya.

Crowned Prince

Rama and Sita were devoted to each other and spent twelve happy years in Ayodhya. They earned the love and respect of its people.

One day Dasharatha called his council of ministers, prominent citizens, rishis and other learned men of his court. He stated to them that he was getting old to carry on the responsibility of ruling his kingdom. In a clear voice that was filled with joy and pride he said, "I therefore wish to crown Rama, my eldest son, as Yuvaraja. Rama has all the qualities and capabilities of a king, to govern Ayodhya."

A loud applause erupted from all those gathered. They commended Dasaratha's wise decision. The people of Ayodhya were delighted that their beloved Rama would be their future king.

Dasharatha called Rama and informed him of his decision. Rama humbly bowed before his father and said, "It is my duty to carry out your every wish, father." Dasharatha, filled with joy, embraced Rama. He ordered the preparations for the crowning ceremony to begin immediately.

Manthara's Evil Counsel

The news of Rama's forthcoming coronation spread quickly throughout Ayodhya. Dasharatha's queens were jubilant at the

king's announcement. The people of Ayodhya were in high spirits, and looked forward to the crowning ceremony.

While the joyous mood prevailed in the entire city, one person was unhappy. She was Manthara, Queen Kaikeyi's maid who was very close to her. In a voice charged with emotion, she asked Kaikeyi, "How can you be happy with Rama being crowned Yuvaraja? Your son Bharata should become the Yuvaraja."

At that time, Bharata was away visiting his uncle Kaikeya. Kaikeyi was a good woman at heart and she loved Rama. But Manthara egged her on. "See how cleverly Dasharatha has arranged for the coronation when Bharata is away at his uncle's house! You must seek the throne for him."

Manthara convinced Kaikeyi that for her own good and that of her son, Bharata should be crowned Yuvaraja.

"But how can I accomplish this, Manthara? Rama is the first born and the throne rightfully is his. How can I have my son Bharata coronated?

Manthara then reminded her of the two boons that Dasharatha had offered her a long time ago.

Old Boons

Once Dasharatha was badly injured in a battle. Sensing danger to his life, Kaikeyi, who was with him, drove him away to a safe place. She nursed his wound and revived him. Overcome with gratitude, Dasharatha granted Kaikeyi two boons which she could use any time.

Now, on the eve of Sri Rama's coronation, Kaikeyi reminded Dasharatha of the two boons he had promised to grant her, years ago.

Kaikeyi told Dasharatha, "You should make Bharata the Yuvaraja. You must send Rama to the forest for fourteen years. These are the two boons I ask for."

Dasaratha was devastated and greatly pained by the enormity of what Kaikeyi had asked him to do. "How can I send my beloved Rama to the forest? How can I bear to be parted from him?" he lamented. But Kaikeyi was unmoved.

Kaikeyi took it upon herself to inform Rama that she had asked for two boons granted by the king long ago. And it was up to Rama to honour his father's promise to her.

Rama was neither unhappy, nor disturbed by the change of events. "I shall fulfill my father's promise to you, mother. I would willingly give away anything to my beloved brother Bharata."

Rama consoled his grief-stricken father saying, "I consider myself fortunate to discharge my duty towards you, father. Do not grieve for me. I am only too happy to honour the promise you have made to mother Kaikeyi."

Rama leaves for Forest

Kausalya swooned when she heard that her beloved son was banished to the forest for fourteen years. Sita and Lakshmana could not bear the thought of being separated from Rama for fourteen years. They too wanted to accompany him to the forest.

Rama had immense love and respect for his parents. He was not at all troubled by the change in fortune. "I have no desire for wealth, power or kingdom. I am happy for Bharata. Bless me father, that I should fulfill your promise," said Rama.

Rama, Lakshmana and Sita dressed themselves in clothes of bark, suitable for life in the jungle. Dasharatha insisted that Sita should retain her jewelry as only Rama was exiled to the forest and she was only accompanying him of her free choice.

The sun set and darkness drew its veil over Ayodhya. Its citizens

agonized over Rama leaving them. Tears flowed copiously down their cheeks as they wept uncontrolled. Inspite of Rama trying to pacify them, they followed his chariot as it sped through the streets of Ayodhya for one last time with Rama seated on it with Lakshmana and Sita.

Soon they reached the border of the kingdom of Kosala. By twilight, they arrived on the banks of then Ganga.

Guha, the chief of the region, got ready a boat for the three of them to cross the river.

Rama took leave of Sumantra who had escorted them to the outskirts of the kingdom. "Return to Ayodhya and take care of my father who suffers great misery, having sent me to the forest."

Sumantra broke down and wept, hearing Rama talk thus. Rama wiped Sumantra's tears and comforted him. "Our family has no friend who is more noble than you, It is your responsibility now to console my father and do whatever you can to lessen his angst," said Rama as he bid farewell to Sumantra.

As Guha also bid farewell to Rama, he said,"This boat will take you safely to the other shore, Sri Rama. Come back safe. We all pray for you."

After crossing the Ganga, Rama called on Sage Bharadwaja who warmly welcomed Dasharatha's sons and Sita. After partaking simple meal with the rishi, they retired to blissful sleep. The following morning, the three of them set out towards Chitrakoota Hill.

Chitrakoota

Sita was enamoured of the environs of Chitrakoota, "How pristine and lovely this forest looks. It is so full of colourful blossoms. Listen to the sweet song of the birds!" Rama was mesmerized by the beauty of the forest.

"How blessed we are to be living among so many rishis and holy men who dwell here in their ashrams," said Rama.

Lakshmana built a mud hut for them. He used bamboo and other jungle materials to make windows and doors.

Repentant Dasharatha

When Sumantra returned to Ayodhya the old king exclaimed "Oh, you have indeed, returned without Rama!" Before Sumantra could reply, the aged king broke into tears.

"Now I'm paying for the sin I committed when I was young, " Dasharatha said, recalling an old incident from his life.

Dasharatha, as a young prince, could shoot at a target out of sight by merely hearing its sound. Once when Dasharatha was out in the wild hunting, he heard a gurgling sound animals make while drinking water. He immediately took aim and hit his target. However, he was shocked when, he heard a human voice scream in pain.

Dasharatha immediately ran in the direction of the sound. He was horrified to see a young ascetic as he lay dying, pierced by the arrow he had shot. It was Shravan Kumar who was taking care of his blind parents in their old age. He had come to the river to fetch water for them. Dasharatha had been hasty in thinking the gurgling sound of water he had heard was caused by an animal.

Dasharatha was filled with remorse for his careless action. He slumped down beside Shravan Kumar and begged forgiveness of the dying young man. As directed by the youngster, he went to the lad's ashram.

He gave Shravan Kumar's parents the water and confessed his deed to them. The parents were shocked and grieved at their young son's untimely demise.

The couple cried over Shravan's body and performed his last rites. Then they said to Dashratha, "You too will endure such grief in your old age as you have now brought upon us! You will suffer the pangs of being parted from your sons, as we do today!" These were their last words before they died broken-hearted.

Dasharatha was disconsolate at being parted from Rama. He raved and ranted, calling out, " Oh Rama, Oh Lakshmana, Rama, Sita, Rama...." His grief was inconsolable. Night fell and at some time in its dark hours, life ebbed out of the King of Ayodhya.

The people of Ayodhya woke up to a gloomy dawn. Dasharatha was gone. The kingdom was without a ruler.

Bharata Returns to Ayodhya

Sage Vasishta, summoned Bharata and Shatrugna who took leave of their uncle and and speedily returned to Ayodhya. Bharata felt very uneasy as he approached the city.

He did not see the usual chirpy crowd on its streets.

As soon as the chariot stopped at the palace, he rushed in to meet his father. He was received by Kaikeyi who informed him of Dasaratha's demise. On hearing this, he broke down with tears streaming down his face.

"The kingdom of Ayodhya is now yours to rule! It is not becoming of a king to mourn in this manner. Get up, my son and prepare yourself to accept the glory that is coming your way." said Kaikeyi.

By now Bharata had learned of everything that had happened in Ayodhya during his absence. Mad with rage, he exploded at his mother:

"You have caused my father's death. You have banished my noble brother to the forest. Do you not know how much I love Rama and look upon him as a father? How could you even imagine I would be happy robbing him of the kingdom that is rightfully his? "

Kaikeyi tried to justify her actions. But nothing that she said consoled Bharata. "I am even ashamed to call you my mother," he said. He wanted to beg Rama for his forgiveness . He wanted to bring Rama back to Ayodhya and offer him his rightful place as its ruler.

Bharata's harsh words brought Kaikeyi to her senses. "Forgive me, son," she pleaded. "I lost my head. I've caused great suffering to all of you."

Brothers meet

Without further delay, Bharata left for the forest to bring back Rama. The queen mothers, Kausalya, Sumitra and Kaikeyi also accompanied him.

From atop a tree, Lakshmana saw Bharata march towards them with his men. Suspicious of Bharata's intent, Lakshmana was all set to fight him.

"Do you not know our Bharata? He knows the way of dharma. It is not to fight or kill that he comes here. He is here to give back the kingdom to me," said Rama. On hearing Rama's words, Lakshmana cringed with shame for having entertained such ignoble thoughts of Bharata.

Rama was happy to see Bharata and he hugged him. He enquired about Dasharatha. When Bharata informed him of their father's demise, Rama wept in sorrow. Rama, Lakshmana and Sita took a dip in the river and offered oblation to the departed king.

Bharata fell at Rama's feet. He asked for forgiveness for what his mother had done and begged him, "Please return home, brother. You alone are worthy of being king of Ayodhya."

"It is my duty that I keep up our father's promise. You too should do as he desired – rule Ayodhya as its king," said Rama.

Kaikeyi also pleaded with Rama to return, saying how much she repented what she had done. But Rama was firm in his resolve to honour his father's words.

Bharata reluctantly agreed to return to Ayodhya without Rama.

He said, "I will go back. But give me your sandals. I will place it on the throne and rule Ayodhya in your name until your return." Bharata returned to Ayodhaya, taking with him Rama's sandals.

Bharata in Nandigram

Upon his return to Ayodhya, Bharata placed Rama's sandals on the throne. "Rama is our king," Bharata told the people of Ayodhya. "Until his return, as his servant, I take charge of protection of the citizens of our kingdom."

Bharata stayed in Nandigrama in the outskirts of Ayodhya, leading the life of an ascetic, just like his brother. He ruled the kingdom from here, helped by able ministers.

Panchavati

After Bharata returned to Ayodhya, the brothers with Sita travelled deeper into the Dandaka forest. They met several rishis. They protected the rishis from the rakshasas who caused them immense suffering.

Later, they moved further down to Panchavati, on the banks of the river Godavari.

"We are surrounded by hills that are so lush with trees," said Rama, looking around.

"Look here, how gently the River Godavari flows with its sparkling blue water! And the sands, shimmering white with the sun's light! Oh, look there, so many deer frolicking with joy!" enthused Sita. She became excited on seeing these animals, birds flying in the sky, flocking on trees and chirping with so much joy.

"Lakshmana, let us stay here. Why don't you look for a place and build us a little ashram here?" asked Rama.

Lakshmana at once set about gathering materials to construct their home. Within no time he raised the mud walls and covered the roof with thatch. They settled down to a cozy existence in their new home.

In Panchavati, they ran into one of Dasharatha's friends. It was Jatayu, the eagle. "Your father was a dear friend. I'm glad you have chosen this place in the forest to live in," said the old bird Jatayu.

Soorpanaka

One day as the brothers and Sita were sitting outside their ashram and chatting, a lovely lady appeared before them.

"I am Soorpanaka, the strong and powerful sister of the mighty Ravana," she announced. Ravana was the ten-headed, demon king of Lanka.

Soorpanaka, though ugly, had magical powers. She had assumed a beautiful form to attract Rama.

Rama showed her due courtesy and told her that he was the son of Dasharatha, living in the forest with his wife Sita and brother Lakshmana.

"Everyone in this forest is afraid of me. But the moment I set eyes on you, I fell in love with you," Soorpanaka said, her voice filled with arrogance.

When Soorpanaka realized Rama was not interested in her, she tried to woo Lakshmana. When Lakshmana too ignored her, she charged towards Sita to hurt her. Lakshmana immediately pulled out his sword and chopped off her nose! Soorpanaka wailed in pain and rushed out of the forest, enraged.

To take revenge on the brothers, she ran to her brother Khara who was the Lord of Janasthana in the Dandaka region. "Brother," she thundered. "Look what the sons of Dasharatha have done to me! Go at once and kill them."

Soorpanaka led Khara and his powerful army to Panchavati. A great battle followed.

Khara's men shot a volley of arrows and darts at Rama. The prince defended them skillfully and killed most of the demons, including Dooshana, Khara's brother. When the battle raged fiercely, as Khara hurled his mace at Rama, the prince shattered it with his arrows. Soon Khara fell dead on the battlefield like the rest of his army.

Ravana Decides to Abduct Sita

Soorpanaka became even more furious when she saw Khara defeated and dead. She went to Ravana to seek revenge against Rama.

"How can you sit here in peace when your land is threatened by two mere mortals?" Soorpanaka asked Ravana. "You must teach them a lesson. Make that lovely Sita your wife. Rama will certainly die of broken heart when his beloved Sita is separated from him." She went on to describe how beautiful Sita was.

The Golden Deer

Ravana made plans to kidnap Sita. To accomplish this he flew across the sea in his aerial car. He was accompanied by his uncle Mareecha.

As soon as they reached Panchavati, Mareecha transformed himself into a golden deer to draw Sita's attention. Ravana hid himself behind the bushes.

Sita was gathering flowers in the forest when she spotted the golden deer with silver spots on its body. She was bewitched by the dazzling beauty of this creature scampering before her. She pointed out the deer to Rama. "Look how playful it is. Get this golden deer for me. We will bring it up as our pet," she begged of Rama.

Rama could not refuse Sita's request. He asked Lakshmana to take care of Sita and went after the deer. The deer frisked and frolicked, moving deeper into the jungle, far away from Rama's ashram. Rama followed. When Rama grew tired of the chase, he shot an arrow at the deer.

The deer fell down on being pierced by Rama's arrow. Mareecha assumed his true form and screamed aloud, imitating Rama's voice: "Ah Sita, ah Lakshmana!" The next moment, Mareecha was dead.

Sita heard the cry, "Ah Sita, ah Lakshmana!" She feared Rama was in danger. Lakshmana tried to convince Sita that this was perhaps a trick played by a rakshasa. Sita disagreed and insisted Rama's life was in danger. She asked Lakshmana to go to his rescue. Lakshmana reluctantly left Sita alone and went in search of Rama. But before leaving, he asked her to be careful. He asked her not to step out of their cottage while he was away.

Ravana Kidnaps Sita

Hidden amidst the thick bushes, Ravana watched all that was happening in Rama's ashram. As soon as he saw Sita alone, he came out of his hiding. He was dressed in saffron clothes and had a staff and pot in each of his hands. He approached Sita.

Sita took him for an ascetic and offered him fruits. The mendicant pushed aside the fruits offered and showed his true form. "I have

come to take you as my wife," he said. "Come, let us go to my kingdom, Lanka."

Ravana grabbed her, set her on his chariot and rose high in the air. Sita was shocked at the sudden turn of events. She cried out to Rama and Lakshmana for help.

"Oh my lord, where are you? Here is this wicked rakshasa who has evil designs on me. Help, help! Oh faithful brother, Lakshmana, rescue me from this demon!"

As Ravana's aerial car rose higher and higher, Sita cried out to all of nature to help her. She cried out to the trees and creatures of the Dandaka forest to inform Rama of her fate.

Jatayu Fights Ravana

Jatayu, heard Sita's wails. He immediately flew in frontof Ravana .

"Oh learned king, you are a protector of people. It is your duty to honour and protect all women."

Jatayu asked Ravana to release Sita but Ravana was in no mood to relent.

Jatayu was old and had no weapons to fight. Yet he could not stand by and watch Ravana take Sita away. "If you are not a coward, get off your chariot and face me!" the old bird challenged the Rakshasa king.

The eagle king tore Ravana's flesh with his talons. He broke the demon's chariot into several pieces and killed the mules harnessed to it. He fought like a true hero. But Ravana was too strong for the ageing bird. He chopped off Jatayu's wings and talons. The bird fell to the ground, grievously wounded.

Sita who looked upon Jatayu as a father, cried in anguish at his plight.

Ravana tightened his grip on Sita and rose in the air with her. He proceeded towards Lanka, flying over mountains and crossing rivers. As Sita looked down, she saw some figures standing on a mountain. With a quick presence of mind, she removed her sash. She bundled a few of her jewels in it and threw it down. She hoped Rama would see her ornaments and get a clue about the direction in which she was taken.

Sita in Lanka

On reaching Lanka, Ravana took Sita to Ashoka Vana. He ordered the rakshasis of his kingdom to keep a watch on her. Ravana tried to entice Sita with all the gold, jewels and wealth in Lanka. Sita was unmoved.

She fearlessly challenged Ravana: "Do not entertain hopes of winning me. It is only a matter of time before Rama comes here to rescue me. You cannot escape the doom and destruction you have brought upon yourself by this evil act."

Sita's unyielding words infuriated Ravana. He gave her twelve months' time to make up her mind to become his wife.

Ashoka Vana was lush with trees, plants and flowers. Deer and peacocks romped freely in the garden. Water lilies and lotuses carpeted its ponds. Ducks and swans gracefully swam in them. Nature's brilliant hues lifted Sita's spirits. It seemed to sustain her faith that her Rama would soon save her from the clutches of evil Ravana.

Jatayu breaks the news to Rama

Meanwhile, at Dandaka, Rama and Lakshmana realized they had been tricked by the demon in the form of the golden deer. They rushed to their ashram only to find Sita missing.

Rama lamented in utter grief. "What I feared has happened! I am sure the rakshasas have made meat of her! We should not have left her alone."

Lakshmana tried to calm Rama. They intensified their search for Sita. They looked for her amidst the dense forests, hills, mountains and river banks surrounding their abode. Fortunately, they spotted the flowers and some golden beads that Sita had scattered when Ravana carried her away. They followed this trail and came upon the wounded Jatayu who was gasping for breath.

Jatayu told Rama that Ravana, the King of Lanka had carried away his dear wife. The wounded bird passed away after delivering this message to Rama.

Rama who regarded Jatayu as his own father, laid the bird to rest and performed his last rites.

Kabanda Directs Rama to Sugreeva

Rama and Lakshmana continued their search for Sita. Their minds oscillated between hope and despair.

As they wondered where to look for Sita, a giant ugly form suddenly appeared before them. He was a demon who had no head or feet. His mouth was on his potlike belly. He had only one eye and that was on his chest! With his two enormous hands he grabbed the brothers.

The brothers acted swiftly and cut off the monster's arms. The monster addressed Rama. "I am Kabandha. I paid the price for my evil deeds with this ugly form. I was cursed by Indra, the king of gods.

Kabandha continued, "Go to the banks of the Pampa River. Meet Sugreeva who lives on the Rishyamooka Hill. Befriend him and he will help you find Sita." Kabandha disappeared after saying this. Sugreeva was the vanara who was driven out of his kingdom by his brother Vali. He took refuge in the Rishyamooka Hill.

Rama and Lakshmana paid heed to Kabandha's words. They proceeded towards the Pampa River to meet Sugreeva.

Sabari

On the way they stopped at the ashram of Sabari, who was an ascetic. She had been waiting for Rama for a long long time. Her Guru,

Mathanga Rishi had told her he would come one day. Patiently she had been waiting for Rama all these years. The brothers spent some time with the ascetic woman and partook fruits she had gathered from the forest. Sabari departed from the world after meeting Rama.

Sugreeva

Sugreeva, who was hiding from his brother-turned-foe Vali, was suspicious of the two strangers coming towards him. He thought they could be Vali's men out to harm him. He asked his trusted lieutenant Hanuman to find out who these two mortals were and what brought them there.

Hanuman, in the guise of a brahmana, approached Rama and Lakshmana. The brothers narrated their story to Hanuman. Hanuman instantly warmed to them. He revealed his identity and took them to Sugreeva.

A cordial friendship sprung between the sons of Dasharatha and Sugreeva. Rama promised Sugreeva help in getting back his lost kingdom from Vali. Sugreeva for his part, agreed to help Rama find Sita.

Vali had of immense strength and was invincible. Yet, Sugreeva challenged his brother to a duel on the strength of Rama's support. Rama hid behind a tree and shot an arrow at Vali that killed him instantly.

Sugreeva was crowned as the king of Kishkinda, the kingdom of the monkeys. He then turned his attention towards making good his promise to Rama. He assembled his vast vaanara army. He made four divisions of his army. He sent one division each to the East, West, North and South, to look for Sita.

Hanuman and Jambavan were part of the team led by Angada.

Rama gave Hanuman his signet ring, saying, "When you find Sita, give her this ring. She will be comforted that you are my messenger."

Search for Sita

The vaanaras spread like ants in all directions looking for Sita. They crossed rivers, leaped upon mountains and combed every forest for Sita. The army that had gone in the East, West and North directions, returned, unsuccessful in their attempt.

Meanwhile, Hanuman and his companions who had headed South, searched the forests and caves of the Vindhya Mountains. They became dejected when they did not get a single clue to Sita's whereabouts. Sitting under a tree on a hill, they started lamenting about their failure.

"We are nearing the time set for us to find Sita.How can we get back to Kishkinda after failing to find her?"

"How can we face Sugreeva and Rama?" asked another Vanara.

Sampati, an old eagle, living on a hill noticed that some Vanaras gathered there seemed to be upset about something.

"It looks like Jatayu lost his life in vain, fighting Ravana in trying to save Sita," joined in another vanara.

At the mention of Jatayu's name, the vulture became alert as Jatayu was his brother living in the far away Chitrakoota.

"How do you know my dear brother Jatayu? You say he is no more! Did Ravana kill him?" Sampati enquired.

Sampati and Jatayu were the sons of Aruna, the god of Dawn. When they were children, they would compete with each other to see who could fly higher in the sky. On one such occasion, when Jatayu got quite close to the Sun, the heat threatened to burn him. Sampati immediately spread his wings to protect Jatayu. In the process Sampati's wings were burnt. He could no longer fly. He fell down on a hill.

Since then, he began to live on the hill because he could not move.

The vanaras recounted to Sampati, how Rama, Lakshmana and Sita came to live in the forest. They told him of Jatayu's heroic efforts to save Sita from Ravana and of how he lost his life.

Sampati was saddened to hear of his brother's demise. He did not want Jatayu's efforts to go in vain. Though Sampati was old and weak, he had very sharp eyesight. He could see things that were very far away. He took a good look across the southern sea and informed the vanaras that Sita was held captive in Lanka, across the sea, surrounded by rakshasis.

The vanaras were jubilant on getting such a big clue from Sampati.

The vanara army had to cross the expansive blue ocean to reach Lanka. They wondered who among them was capable of making such a huge leap. While each monkey hero boasted of his power, the one who could achieve the rare deed of leaping over the ocean was keeping quiet, sitting aloof from others. He was Hanuman, the son of Vayu, the wind god.

Hanuman

When Hanuman was a child, he soared high in the sky to catch the Sun thinking it was a juicy fruit. Indra, the king of the devas feared Hanuman would snatch the Sun. He threw his weapon, the thunderbolt, at the leaping child. Hanuman's jaw broke and he fell on a mountain. Seeing his son injured, Hanuman's father Vayu was enraged. He stopped his movements and became still. There was no air for anyone to breathe. All creatures became breathless and felt suffocated.

All the gods begged Vayu to cast away his anger. Brahma and Indra appeared before Hanuman and gave him boons. "No weapon can kill you. You will be immortal," they said.

Child Hanuman was very mischievous. The sages in the forest threw a spell on him so that he would not know his own power

until some one reminded him of it. Jambavan, the wise bear, who was aware of Hanuman's power asked the monkeys to surround the Vanara hero. "Hanuman, you alone can leap across the ocean," said Jambavan, reminding him of his immense power. Other monkeys started chanting, "Yes, Hanuman, you can, Hanuman you can."

As the chanting grew louder, Hanuman grew in size. Soon he stood tall like a palm tree. The earth was squeezed as he pressed his feet on the hill.

Hanuman Leaps across the sea

In one quick move, Hanuman lifted himself from the mountain peak. The trees that got uprooted too were thrown up in the sky. He was soon air-borne, soaring far and high, and on his way to Lanka.

When he was half way down to Lanka, Mount Mynaka, Vayu's friend, who resided in the ocean, stopped Hanuman. He asked Hanuman to rest a while on its summit before proceeding to Lanka.

Hanuman politely said, "No, thanks. Rama's work comes first," as he flew past Mynaka.

Suddenly, Hanuman felt some force pulling him down. It was a sea monster that held on to Hanuman's shadow on the water. The monster challenged Hanuman to enter her mouth and come out alive, if he could. Hanuman agreed and grew to enormous size. To swallow him, the monster opened her mouth wide. Hanuman suddenly shrunk to the size of a mosquito, entered her mouth and flew out alive.

Hanuman in Lanka

Hanuman soon reached Lanka. He assumed his normal size and perched himself on a tree to survey Ravana's city. It stood splendorous on Mount Trikuta. A gigantic fort encircled Lanka which had lavish palaces, mansions and beautiful gardens.

Oh Rama ...
My Rama ...

Just then the guardian angel of Lanka stopped him. Hanuman gave her a push and sent her reeling. She gave way to Hanuman. It was prophesied that when she was overpowered by a monkey, it would spell doom to the city of Ravana.

There were armed guards and soldiers everywhere in the fort city. They took no notice of a monkey passing by.

Hanuman roamed the palace complex in search of Sita. He peeped into every chamber and every apartment hoping to see Sita. But she was now here to be seen.

Just then Hanuman's roving eyes sighted an area of Lanka he had not searched. It was the magnificent Ashoka Vana, surrounded by a high wall.

Hanuman, without further delay, hopped on to the wall. Dusk fell as he jumped on to a tree that was dense with branches and dark green leaves. His eyes searched every corner of Ashoka Vana for Sita.

Hanuman caught sight of a woman sitting under a tree, surrounded by ugly rakshasis. She looked so divinely beautiful in total contrast to the rakshasis sitting around her. Hanuman's heart told him he had found Rama's wife Sita.

Hanuman began to softly sing the story of Rama and of how his beloved wife Sita was abducted by the wicked Ravana. Hearing the story of Rama, Sita was delighted and scared at the same time. "Who could this be who is singing beloved Rama's story? Could it be a rakshasa trying to trick me?"

Sita looked all around to locate the source of the voice. As she looked up, Hanuman jumped down from the tree and stood before her. He said he was Rama's emissary. He related to her the pangs of pain Rama suffered after losing her. He narrated how Rama sought Sugreeva's help in finding her. Sita was overjoyed at this meeting with Hanuman . "Mother, Rama asked me to give this to you as proof of my being a messenger from him," said Hanuman, as he handed Rama's signet ring to her.

She took the ring from Hanuman and pressed it to her eyes . It was as if she was seeing Rama himself.

"I want Rama to come here soon and rescue me from Ravana. Only two months remain of the twelve months the demon has given me," said Sita to Hanuman.

"Rest assured Mother, Rama will surely save you from this evil rakshasa soon," Hanuman comforted Sita.

As Hanuman took leave of Sita, she handed him a piece of her jewelry, saying: "Rama would be happy to see this as proof of your having met me. Give it to him when you reach Kishkinda."

Hanuman on rampage

Hanuman wanted to create fear in the minds of the Rakshasas. He started uprooting trees in the Ashoka Vana. The sleeping Rakshasis woke up, hearing the noises around them. As Hanuman pounced on them, they ran to their king. "There is a huge monkey that has ruined our lovely Ashoka Vana. We also saw him talk to Sita."

Ravana was livid with anger when he heard this. "Kill this monstrous monkey," he ordered his guards.

Hanuman attacked the soldiers and killed them all. Hanuman shook the city of Lanka with loud roars that echoed throughout the region. The rakshasas trembled with fear. Ravana's son Aksha came to battle Hanuman.

Hanuman charged against Aksha's chariot and smashed it to pieces. Aksha was undaunted. He rose in the air, bow and arrow in hand. The battled raged fiercely in the air. Hanuman delivered the final blow and the young hero fell dead.

A fierce battle ensued between Indrajit and Hanuman. Hanuman rose in the sky becoming bigger than ever. Indrajit used the much feared Brahmastra against Hanuman and bound him with it.

The rakshasas shouted in joy at the fall of Hanuman. They tied him with ropes, and dragged him through the streets of Lanka to Ravana's court.

Hanuman surveyed Ravana's court as he stood before the demon king. Hanuman gazed at the rich ornamentation of his court, and at Ravana himself.

"It does not befit a king of your stature and learning, to carry off another man's wife and hold her captive," Hanuman told Ravana.

"Return Sita with all honour to Rama and seek his forgiveness. Else, Rama is bound to destroy you and your clan."

Ravana was outraged by Hanuman's words. He ordered his men to set Hanuman's tail on fire.

Lanka up in Flames

The guards obeyed Ravana. They doused Hanuman's tail with oil and set it ablaze. They then took him in procession along the streets of their city. Hanuman increased his size and began jumping from tree to tree, building to building. He set fire to whatever came his way. Everything in Lanka, except the tree in Ashoka Vana under which Sita sat, was on fire.

Hanuman was satisfied with what he had accomplished. He doused the fire on his tail in the sea water. He was ready to fly back to Rama

with the good tidings. Before leaving Lanka, he once again made his salutations to Sita and took her blessings.

The vanaras were beside themselves with joy when Hanuman rejoined them. When he told them he had found Sita, they broke into a dance. The vanaras proceeded to Kishkinda to give Rama the joyous news of having found Sita.

Rama Overwhelmed with Joy

"I have seen Mother Sita. I met your pure and divine queen. I spoke to the graceful lady who is your wife. I bring you good tidings. Mother Sita is safe even though she is in the midst of the cruel rakshasis," said Hanuman bowing to Rama.

Tears flowed down Rama's cheeks as Hanuman narrated his meeting with Sita and the events of Lanka.

"Mother Sita wants you to rescue her from Ravana as soon as possible. She gave me her crest jewel to hand over to you as a

proof of my meeting her." Saying this, Hanuman gave Rama the ornament Sita had given him.

More tears flowed from Rama's eyes as he saw the piece of jewelry. He embraced Hanuman, saying, "Blessed are you, son of Vayu. You have achieved the impossible!"

Vibheeshana Advices Ravana

Rama and the vanara force were elated at Hanuman's feat. Soon Rama and Lakshmana left Kishkinda. They headed the Vanara Sena and proceeded south.

Meanwhile, Ravana called an assembly of his ministers. He wanted to assess the threat posed by Rama.

His ministers, however, were brimming with confidence. They said, "Our warriors can deal with Rama. We have weapons to crush anyone who challenges you."

While Ravana's ministers praised him, Vibheeshana disagreed with them. "Brother, it is indeed nice to hear what these people say. But it is not good or sensible advice to act upon. Rama had done us no harm. If he fought and killed our men in Dandaka forest, he did so only in self defence. Yet you carried his wife away. This is a grave sin. Even now it is not too late to make amends. Restore Sita to Rama and he will forgive you."

Vibheeshana's pleas to Ravana fell on deaf ears. "I will neither restore Sita nor ask Rama for forgiveness," roared Ravana, his eyes turning red with rage. "I will fight Rama in battle."

Kumbhakarna Stands by Ravana

Kumbhakarna, another younger brother of Ravana, agreed with Vibheeshana. "You did not act right in carrying Sita away," he said. Yet, if you have made up your mind, I shall fight the sons of Dasharatha and slay them." said Kumbhakarna who was known for his extraordinary strength. "Victory will be yours, brother."

Vibheeshana, however, was firm in his resolve. He made one final effort to make Ravana see sense. "Our defeat is certain if we fight

Rama. I beg you brother, return Sita. She rightfully belongs to Rama and no one else. Save yourself from this sinful act and also our clan from destruction."

Ravana was unyielding. "You talk like a coward, Vibheeshana. If I act upon your words, it would only bring dishonor to our race."

Vibheeshana realized there was no place for him in Lanka. Ravana had no ears for good council. Vibheeshana did not wish to take sides with the wrong and unjust. He renounced all his possessions and left Lanka to join hands with Rama.

Preparations for War

Rama had reached the shore of the southern sea where Vibheeshana sought refuge in him.

Rama prayed to the God of the ocean to grant a safe passage to Lanka so that his army could march to the city of Ravana.

Rama prayed for three days. When there was no response, Rama got upset with the sea and picked up his bow. He threatened to dry up the sea by invoking powerful astras. Varuna, the Lord of the ocean rose from the sea and pacified Rama. He pointed out that one had to respect nature's laws. He advised Rama to build a bridge to Lanka.

The Vanara hero Nala, the son of Vishwakarma, came forward to build the bridge across the sea. Thousands of vanaras chipped in

their bit to construct it. A small squirrel carried pebbles and small stones to fill in the gap between boulders piled in the sea. Overcome by gratitude, Rama patted the little squirrel, causing three stripes to appear on the animal's back.

The huge vanara army marched on the long bridge to Lanka. Hanuman carried Rama on his shoulder and Angada carried Lakshmana.

Before mounting an attack, Rama sent Angada with a message to Ravana. "Oh King, your end is approaching. Rama is at your fort gate, ready to fight you. If you love your life, if you are repentant for your evil deed, restore Sita to Rama and beg his forgiveness. He is merciful."

Ravana was angered by Angada's words. He ordered his men to kill Rama's envoy.

As Ravana's guards made to seize Angada, the monkey rose high in the sky. He lifted the two guards, one in each hand, soared high and flung them down.

The War Begins

The battle between the two sides began in all ferocity. It raged unabated through the day and continued into the night. Horses galloped with riders and elephants marched with soldiers mounted on them. All kinds of weapons flew in every direction, each meeting its target. Fallen soldiers cried loud in pain and agony. Lanka's fertile, brown earth turned red with the blood bath. Both sides witnessed heavy loss of life.

At one point of time during the battle, Indrajit shot serpent darts at Rama and Lakshmana. Bound by them, the brothers fell down, immobile. However, Garuda, the King of birds descended on the site of the battle. At the sight of Garuda, serpents which had wound round the brothers fled. The two brothers thanked Garuda.

On another occasion, Lakshmana was mortally wounded and Rama was heart- broken. Hanuman flew to the Himalayas and flew back

with Sanjeevani mountain containing the life saving Sanjeevani herbs. Lakshmana was revived with the medicinal herbs.

Kumbhakarna pressed into the battle

A great battle followed. One by one, Ravana lost most of his great warriors. Only one man could save the Rakshasas. It was the sleeping giant, Kumbhkarna. But he would sleep for six long months at a stretch and would be wakeful for just one day. Ravana ordered that his sleeping brother be awakened.

Hundreds of people were sent to wake up the giant. As he breathed in, they were sucked into his enormous nose and they would be thrown out of the cave-like nose of the giant when he breathed out.

Keeping out of way of his breathing, they clapped, beat drums and gongs, and blew conches. Deaf to all the noise around him, Kumbhakarna slept. They jabbed him with sticks, they pounded on his chest. They made elephants walk on the sleeping giant.

The giant continued to snore. At last the aroma of food which was getting ready floated in and tickled his nose. Soon the giant woke up to the delicious smell of the food he loved. The attendants waited patiently till Kumbhkarna had his fill. With his stomach full, the giant

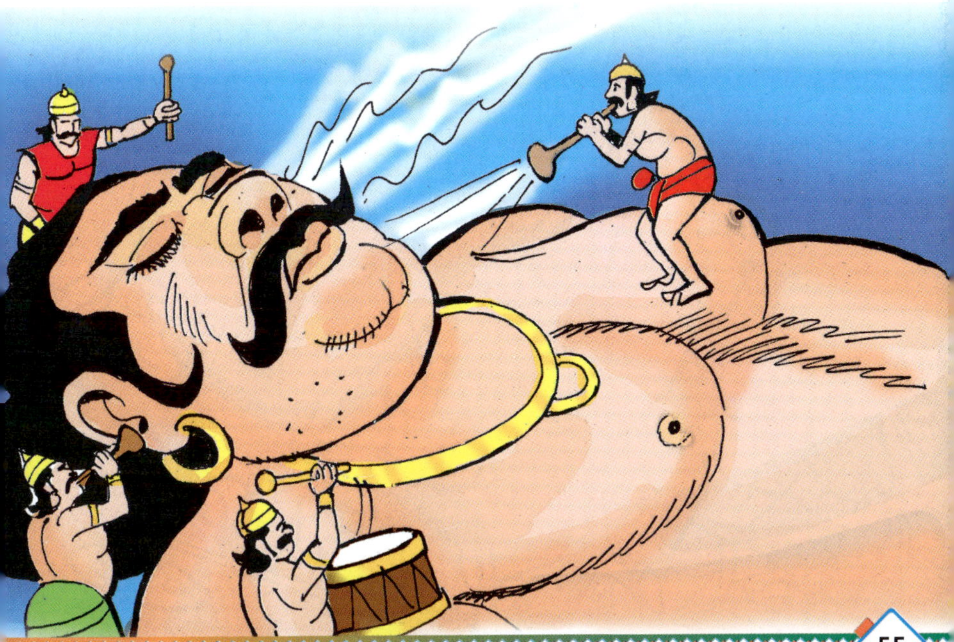

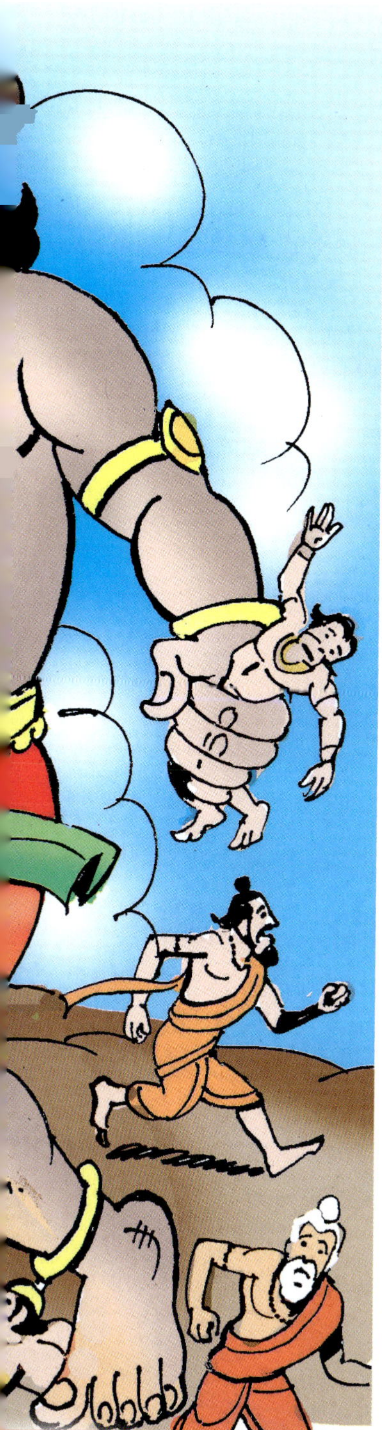

belched with satisfaction and only then he was told that Ravana was waiting for him.

Kumbhakrana met Ravana and assured him he would destroy the enemies and strode into the battle field. His very sight frightened the monkey heroes. They ran helter skelter as the giant grabbed those he could lay his hands on and gobbled them down.

Ignoring Lakshmana who was itching to fight him, Kumbhakarna took on Rama. A terrible battle ensued. After the sea-saw battle, at last the giant fell to Rama's arrow with a thud.

Furious at the death of his uncle, Indrajit, Ravana's son charged forth. Single handedly he destroyed thousands of monkeys and threatened to wipe out Rama's entire army. At last he fell to Lakshmana.

Rama Defeats Ravana

Ravana's best men were all dead. He finally faced Rama in battle. It was the battle of two giants. Indra had sent his chariot to Rama for his use. Rama's arrow found its mark as it knocked down Ravana's head. But to Rama's surprise, next moment, another head grew in its place and Ravana was roaring like a wounded lion. Rama sent forth another arrow to knock down Ravana's head but, as before, another head grew in no time and Ravana continued to fight.

This happened ten times. At last, Rama used the Brahmastra which pierced Ravana's chest. Ravana's bow slipped from his hand and the demon king fell dead. He was vanquished.

All the devas, gods and sages rejoiced at Rama's victory. They showered flowers on him.

There was great jubilation among the vanaras. Rama profusely thanked them for all the help they had rendered. He then crowned Vibheeshana king of Lanka.

Fire Ordeal

The jubilant Sita, with her heart beating for Rama, approached her husband. Rama's heart was full of love for his beloved but his words were harsh. Rama told Sita that he vindicated his honour by killing the Rakshasa who had abducted his wife. But could he take home with him the wife who had spent a year in another man's abode?

Sita was shocked to hear Rama speak in this manner. Sita did not expect this from her beloved Rama. She asked Lakshmana to prepare fire. Sita joined hands in salutation to all gods and addressed fire god, Agni. "Oh Agni" said Sita, " Rama doubts my love for him. You are witness to truth. You know my heart beats for Rama all the time. Take me." With these words, Sita stepped into the blazing fire.

The next moment, Agni deva emerged from the flame, escorting Sita. "Rama, Sita is pure at heart. All the time she thinks only of you. Accept her."

Rama's eyes brimmed with tears. He drew Sita close to him. "Did I ever entertain any doubt on your love for me? I know in my heart you are ever pure. But I wanted the whole world to know it."

Rama Crowned King

Sita was happily united with Rama. Together with Lakshmana, they ascended the Pushpaka Viman, the aerial car and sped to Ayodhya. Their years of exile were complete. Bharata who was eagerly awaiting Rama's return, ran to him and embraced him.

The city of Ayodhya was drowned in joy from Rama's home coming. Rama was crowned king in a grand celebration.